My First Animal Library

Bison

by Cari Meister

Bullfrog Books

Ideas for Parents and Teachers

Bullfrog Books let children practice reading informational text at the earliest reading levels. Repetition, familiar words, and photo labels support early readers.

Before Reading

- Discuss the cover photo. What does it tell them?
- Look at the picture glossary together. Read and discuss the words.

Read the Book

- "Walk" through the book and look at the photos. Let the child ask questions. Point out the photo labels.
- Read the book to the child, or have him or her read independently.

After Reading

- Prompt the child to think more. Ask: Have you ever seen a bison? Were you surprised by its size?

Bullfrog Books are published by Jump!
5357 Penn Avenue South
Minneapolis, MN 55419
www.jumplibrary.com

Library of Congress Cataloging-in-Publication Data

Names: Meister, Cari, author.
Title: Bison / by Cari Meister.
Description: Minneapolis, MN : Jump!, Inc., 2018.
Series: My first animal library | Series: Bullfrog books | Includes index. | Audience: Ages 5 to 8.
Audience: Grades K to 3.
Identifiers: LCCN 2017040016 (print)
LCCN 2017043343 (ebook)
ISBN 9781624967511 (ebook)
ISBN 9781624967504 (hardcover : alk. paper)
Subjects: LCSH: American bison--Juvenile literature.
Classification: LCC QL737.U53 (ebook) | LCC QL737.U53 M428 2018 (print) | DDC 599.64/3—dc23
LC record available at https://lccn.loc.gov/2017040016

Editor: Jenna Trnka
Book Designer: Leah Sanders

Photo Credits: Eric Isselee/Shutterstock, cover, 1, 22, 24; Leena Robinson/Shutterstock, 3; Stephan Hermannsdrfer/EyeEm/Getty, 4; neelsky/Shutterstock, 5; Shannon T/Shutterstock, 6–7; Arnold Media/Getty, 8–9; Jim Brandenburg/Minden Pictures/SuperStock, 10, 23mr; Sharon Day/Shutterstock, 11, 23tr; ottavianoserena/Shutterstock, 12–13; blickwinkel/Schmidbauer/Alamy, 14–15, 23tl; Mark Weber/Getty, 16–17, 23ml, 23bl; Cybernesco/iStock, 18; Michelle Holihan/Shutterstock, 19; SageElyse/iStock, 20–21; Ad_hominem/Shutterstock, 23br.

Printed in the United States of America at Corporate Graphics in North Mankato, Minnesota.

Table of Contents

Big and Brown

What is that animal eating grass?

It is brown.

It is shaggy.

It is a bison!

A bison is big.

How big?

It is the biggest animal in North America!

Wow!

They were
once hunted.

Now they are
protected.

Most live in parks.

9

Bison live in herds.
They roam.

10

They graze.

Males are called bulls.

They fight.

For what?

The cows.

Their horns crash!
Watch out!

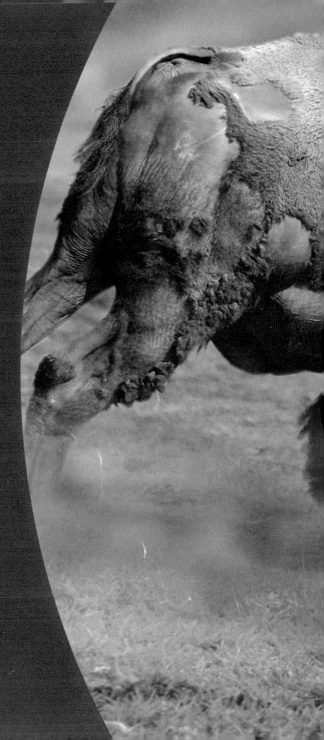

horn

calf

Cows have one calf at a time.

Look how small!

It has brown fur, too.

Bison fur is thick.
It keeps them warm.

18

Even in snow.

See the hump?

It helps the bison
move its head.

It plows through snow.

It finds food!

hump

Parts of a Bison

horns
A bison uses its horns to fight.

hump
The hump on a bison's shoulders is made of muscle. It helps the bison use its head as a snowplow in winter.

fur
Thick fur keeps bison warm in winter. They shed their thick fur in summer.

tail
Bison have a short tail with a furry tuft.

Picture Glossary

bulls
Adult male bison.

graze
To eat grass.

calf
A baby bison.

herds
Large groups of animals that live and travel together.

cows
Adult female bison.

North America
The continent that includes the United States, Canada, Mexico, and Central America.

Index

To Learn More

Learning more is as easy as 1, 2, 3.

1) Go to www.factsurfer.com

2) Enter "bison" into the search box.

3) Click the "Surf" button to see a list of websites.

With factsurfer.com, finding more information is just a click away.